Time to Celebrate!

By Frieda Wishinsky
and Cynthia Benjamin

CELEBRATION PRESS
Pearson Learning Group

Contents

Introduction

   For many years people all over the world have celebrated special holidays. This book tells about some of those celebrations. Some of them honor events in a country's history. Others let people give thanks or show respect. All the celebrations give people a chance to have a great time together.

Cinco de Mayo

Mexicans and Mexican Americans celebrate a holiday called Cinco de Mayo. In Spanish this means "fifth of May." This holiday celebrates a famous battle in Mexican history.

The Battle of Puebla

People celebrating Cinco de Mayo often wear traditional Mexican clothes. ▶

In 1862 thousands of French soldiers began marching through Mexico. They thought they would quickly beat the Mexican army.

They were wrong. The Mexican army did not have nearly as many soldiers or weapons. Yet on May 5, 1862, they beat the French army at the Battle of Puebla.

The Battle of Puebla was fought in Puebla, Mexico.

Later, Americans helped the Mexican army drive the French out of Mexico. Today Mexicans and Mexican Americans celebrate Cinco de Mayo to remember the victory. The day is filled with parties, dancing, and speeches.

On Cinco de Mayo many children take part in street parades.

Chinese New Year

Not everyone celebrates New Year's Day on January 1. In the Chinese calendar the first day of the year falls between the middle of January and the middle of February. Many people around the world celebrate Chinese New Year in many ways.

This girl is wearing red silk clothes for Chinese New Year. Many Chinese people believe that red brings joy and happiness.

The Chinese New Year celebration began more than 4,000 years ago. The celebration let farmers know when the spring planting should begin. Today Chinese people all over the world celebrate Chinese New Year.

Inside the dragon costume dancers turn the dragon's body and make its eyes blink.

During Chinese New Year children receive red envelopes with money inside them.

Chinese New Year lasts for fifteen days. On the first day everyone wears new clothes. People dance through the streets. Many parade in dragon or lion costumes.

Chinese New Year ends with the Lantern Festival. Shopkeepers hang lighted paper lanterns outside their shops. People carry lanterns through the streets in parades.

Mother's Day

In March, April, and May, people in many countries honor their mothers. Some history experts believe the first Mother's Days were festivals held in ancient Greece and Rome.

On Mother's Day many children around the world make cards for their mothers.

Hundreds of years ago people in England celebrated a holiday called Mothering Sunday. The holiday took place in March or April. Workers would visit their mothers and give them small gifts or cakes.

Mothering Sunday is still celebrated in the United Kingdom today.

Many people celebrate Mother's Day thanks to a woman named Anna Jarvis. She wanted the United States to name a day to honor mothers. She wrote many letters to people in the U.S. government. In 1914 the second Sunday in May was named Mother's Day. That Sunday is also Mother's Day in Canada, Australia, Japan, and other countries.

N'cwala

Every February a harvest festival takes place in eastern Zambia, a country in Africa. The festival is called N'cwala or "first fruits." It is celebrated by the

Ngoni dancers travel to the festival.

Ngoni, a group of people who live in the area. On N'cwala the Ngoni also honor the day they first settled in Zambia in 1835.

AFRICA

Zambia

Zambia

Mutenguleni

Map Key

◉ Village

N
W — E
S

The N'cwala festival takes place in the village of Mutenguleni.

Dancing has always been an important part of N'cwala. The finest dancers from twelve villages take part. They practice on the day before the celebration.

This Ngoni boy wears a traditional costume when he dances.

zebra-hair headdress

n'kholi (wooden stick)

cowhide and fur shield

The Ngoni women make a circle around the dancers.

Each group of dancers performs a warrior dance. At the same time the Ngoni women clap their hands and sing. Their songs tell how strong and fierce the dancers are.

It is a great honor to dance at N'cwala.

Thanksgiving in Canada

Many people celebrate to give thanks for what they have. In Canada a day of thanks happens in October. That is the time of the country's autumn harvest.

Some Canadian towns hold autumn fairs around Thanksgiving.

Sir Martin Frobisher explored Baffin Island and other Arctic areas of northern Canada.

The first Canadian Thanksgiving took place in 1578. Sir Martin Frobisher, an explorer from England, landed on an island in northern Canada. He held a celebration to give thanks for his safe voyage. Many years later, in 1957, the Canadian government named the second Monday in October Thanksgiving Day.

Thanksgiving in the United States

In the United States Thanksgiving is celebrated on the fourth Thursday in November. It has been a national holiday since 1941. Thanksgiving was first celebrated long before that, however. The Pilgrims, settlers from England, held a celebration of thanks in 1621.

Many Americans eat turkey on Thanksgiving.

The Pilgrims had built a settlement in Massachusetts the year before. Native Americans in the area taught the Pilgrims how to hunt, fish, and plant crops. The Pilgrims celebrated their rich harvest with a three-day feast. They invited their Native American neighbors to thank them for their help.

The 1621 Thanksgiving feast

Australia Day

Australia Day is Australia's largest national celebration. It is held on January 26. Australians celebrate their country's past and future on Australia Day.

People crowd the streets to watch Australia Day parades.

Since 1946 Australia Day has been a holiday throughout the country. Each year on that day many people become new Australian citizens. Awards are given to Australians who have helped their communities in an important way.

On Australia Day boat races are held on Sydney Harbour.

Many events are held on Australia Day. People march in parades. Performers celebrate the history of Australia's people. There are sporting events and musical shows. Many people have a great time on Australia Day.

Many Australian families celebrate the day by going to the beach.

A Year of Celebrations

When are the holidays you celebrate?

	Celebration	Date
	Chinese New Year	between January 21 and February 21
	Australia Day	January 26
	N'cwala	February 24
	Mothering Sunday	sometime in March or April
	Cinco de Mayo	May 5
	Mother's Day in many countries	second Sunday in May
	Thanksgiving in Canada	second Monday in October
	Thanksgiving in the United States	fourth Thursday in November

Index